I Am

D.I.V.A.

Destined   Integrity   Victorious   Anointed

I Am

D.I.V.A.

Destined   Integrity   Victorious   Anointed

...that's who God
"*called*" me to be, and MUCH More!"

LaDonna Michelle'

PTP
Pure Thoughts Publishing LLC

The opinions expressed by the author are not necessarily those of ReadersMagnet, LLC. All Bible verses in this book are from the New King James Version.

ISBN: 978-1-943409-76-1

Reviews

"I Am D.I.V.A" challenges us to see ourselves as God has created us to be in Christ Jesus. This book has been designed for the person who is struggling with the process of being transformed into the image of Christ while gaining victory during spiritual warfare. Once we embrace the truth of who God says we are, we are empowered to maximize our potential and fulfill our God-given destiny. Lady LaDonna's story reminds us that there is never a victory without a battle, and the Word of God declares, "And they overcame him by the blood of the Lamb and by the word of their testimony…" (Revelation 12:11 NKJ)

— Dr. Sherry Gaither, Pastor
Empowerment Network International

Revelation 12:10-12 tells us of this heavenly pronouncement: "Now salvation, and strength, and The kingdom of our God and the power of His Christ have come" into the earth. As God would have it, I AM DIVA is a living testimony that Lady LaDonna "overcame the accuser" of our souls, "by the blood of the Lamb and by the word of [her] testimony," which she now shares freely.

May each reader, young and older, whether female or male, find encouragement in Lady's powerfully intimate sharing and be reminded that they too are free to live the life God purposed—all to God's glory!

— Elder Ada M. White Taylor, D.Min.,
Contributing Editor

"I AM D.I.V.A is a book for anyone who's been vulnerable and made mistakes throughout this journey called life. The book is filled with stories of secrets, sadness, devastation, insecurities, dysfunction, loneliness, life as Preacher's Kid (PK) but it is also a story about an Overcomer. The book begins with a Powerful statement that we can all relate to, "It has not always been a beautiful story: it's been a journey!" This book will leave you feeling encouraged, inspired, uplifted and knowing that you can "run and see" what the end is going to be. I highly recommend this book, I AM D.I.V.A, because the author, LaDonna Michellé is passionate about helping others heal and overcome the pain of their past. This book has reminded me, I AM D.I.V.A., Destined, Integral, Victorious, and Anointed."

— **Mrs. Jafora Fox, MBA, Phd Student**
Business Strategist

"Lady LaDonna's Book D.I.V.A. is encouraging and uplifting. It will bring joy and you may even shed some tears. You will see that you are not the only one that has gone through some painful situations in your life, but she lets you know that you are somebody, I Am D.I.V.A. I have a testimony, I made it, and I survived. Now I can help someone else not to give up, and you can see that I am not in this alone. Lady LaDonna's book is all that and more."

— **Pastor Beverly Crawford,**
Grammy-nominated and Multi
Stellar Gospel Music Award Winner

"Words of Wisdom… Leaving a Legacy"

From Mom

Love yourself first! Sometimes it may be the hardest thing to do because of failed situations in life.

Don't be a gopher! If a person says that they love you, they will not ask you to sin against God, our Creator. Wanting to "fit in" will cause you to stumble and veer off of your predestined path. Stay the course.

Read and Live in the Word of God - it has every life's tool in there so that we can live a successful life in Him. Keep your eyes on Him. It is also very important to remember your home training.

Don't try to "fit in" where you don't belong. God has a specific assignment and platform for you, you and only you my dear.

No matter what people say about you, what really matters is what God says to and about YOU, and be very careful what you say about yourself!

Never Settle! Never underestimate the "calling and gifts" that God has established in you, even before the foundation of this world.

My dear woman, never under value who you are... God makes no mistakes! May the Heavenly Father's divine Love, Grace, Protection, Mercy and Wisdom be with you always.

D.I.V.A., remain prayerful and watchful at all times.

Pastor Gloria

Psalm 17:8 (NIV)

"Keep me as the apple of your eye; hide me in the shadow of your wings..."

Matthew 7:12 (KJV)

"Therefore, all things whatsoever ye would that men should do to you: do ye even so to them: for this is the law and the prophets."

1 Peter 2:9 (NIV)

"But you are a chosen people, a royal priesthood, a holy nation, God's special possession, that you may declare the praise of him who called you out of darkness into his wonderful light..."

I chuckled and smiled in my sleep the night before as I dreamt about this beautiful song. Waking the next morning, I heard it playing in my head over and over, listening intently, with tears running down my cheeks, I began singing along:

I've had my share of life's ups and downs
But fate's been kind, the downs have been few
I guess you could say that I've been lucky
Well, I guess you could say that it's all because of you

"...If anyone should ever write my life
story For whatever reason there might be
Oh, you'll be there between each line of pain And glory
Cause you're [Jesus] the best thing that ever
Happened to me..."

Best Thing That Ever Happened to Me

Gladys Knight & The Pips
Album: "Imagination" (1973)
Lyrics licensed and provided by LyricFind
© Sony/ATV Music Publishing LLC,
Writer/s: JAMES D. WEATHERLY
Publisher: Sony/ATV Music Publishing LLC,
Universal Music Publishing Group,
Kobalt Music Publishing Ltd.

Table of Contents

I Am D.I.V.A.

I Am Destined! I Am Integrity!
I Am Victorious! I Am Anointed!

. . . that's who God "called" me to
be, and MUCH more!

I humbly dedicate this book, first and foremost, to God, my Father, and Jesus Christ, who truly is my ROCK. Without Him, there would be no me. I'm glad He created and predestined me. For that, I am grateful.

I also dedicate this book to my beautiful late Grandmother Devonza. "Mother," your true wisdom, care and love for family and others has taught me valuable life's lessons, thank you.

To my prayer warrior, intercessor, angel and friend, my beautiful mother (Pastor Gloria), the epitome of grace and love.

Mom, your example of strength, wisdom, love and prayer mean more to me than words could ever express, I love you dearly.

To my family - uncles, aunts, siblings, cousins, nieces and nephews, thank you for the authentic family love.

To my beautiful children and grandkids, you have changed my life forever. For that, I will never be the same again. I am so proud of you guys, Mommie "G-Momma" loves you dearly, to the moon and beyond!

Finally, I dedicate this book to women all over the world. From young girls growing into

womanhood and to women who have stood the test of time, my hope is that you will be blessed, encouraged and empowered as a result of this literary encounter.

Acknowledgment

A work of this magnitude could never be a solo effort. Therefore, I must give honor where it is due. I am beyond grateful for the guidance of the Holy Spirit, which guides us into all truth, according to John 16:13.

I would also like to acknowledge the undying support of my publisher Dr. Marita Kinney and the Pure Publishing team, family, children, friends, prayer warriors, vocational teachers, Florida college professors, Atlanta seminary professors, supporters, my church family, ministry, and music colleagues as well as my production team.

To my Pastor Dr. Jamal H. Bryant, New Birth Missionary Baptist Cathedral, Stonecrest, Georgia, thank you for your continuous commitment for greater greatness in the body of Christ. Your preaching and your teachings are profound and are most relevant and prolific across all spectrums.

Thank you, New Birth Missionary Baptist Cathedral, Stonecrest Georgia leadership for 24 plus years of biblical teachings and discipleship from the founder the Late Apostle Eddie L. Long, truly a gift to the world. And to First Lady Elder Vanessa Long, for your gentle spirit and powerful words of wisdom.

I'd also like to acknowledge the lovely Dr. Sherry Gaither, my former Beulah Heights Seminary College professor.

To friends Cheryl McDowell, Pastor Alonia Jones, Rev. Shalise Steele-Young and others - you ladies are heaven sent.... oh, the many girl chats! To one of my coaches and intercessors Elder Dr. Ada Taylor, you are one-of-a-kind. Your words and biblical knowledge have a way of changing one's mindset in the most gentlest way.

Thank everyone who played a part in this endeavor out front and behind the closed doors in educational, secular and gospel arena, I am grateful to you all! We have displayed again that firm

and steady teamwork will make a dream and vision come into its full fruition.

Thank you for supporting our dream all the way to the end.

And to all the former ministries and community leaders from my childhood, thank you for providing foundational teachings and ministry tools that advanced my Christian journey.

Where are my D.I.V.A.s?

To every D.I.V.A. of all languages, ethnicities, doctrines, beliefs, shapes and sizes, I say: live in your empowerment, self-love, self-awareness - destiny. For it is imperative to find our rightful place and stand firmly in that place! It is our journey of life.

From the woman serving as a corporate CEO, to the woman managing her home, to the woman who may find herself in a state of homelessness and disparity. To the woman suffering with camouflaged insecurities and low self-esteem. To the woman experiencing toxicity through emotional, sexual and or manipulative abuse through personal relationships by accepting love from all the wrong places. To the woman who has dealt with separation and a failed marriage. And even to the woman who appears to have it all, this is written to YOU.

My prayer is that these words will resonate with and transform every woman who is yearning to find, understand, and fulfill her purpose and destiny. In my continual walk with Him, the Lord has revealed to me a clearer understanding as to the meaning of "I AM."

May each of you find endless love, joy, hope, faith, wisdom and encouragement in your most celebrated moments and even in your tough and broken places. Know this: bad experiences cannot and will not stop you from walking in your *Greater.*

Be reminded D.I.V.A.: you are *Destined* in the most *Integral* way; you are *Victorious,* and you are *Anointed! ~ I Am D.I.V.A.*!

D - DESTINED

I - INTEGRITY

V - VICTORIOUS

A - ANOINTED

Reared in the church, I believed that before being formed in my mother's womb, I was called into existence in this world. . . before I even thought about birthday gifts and birthday celebrations, I was created and predestined for greater greatness! You, you and you were created and predestined for greater! Growing up as a preacher's kid (PK), I often heard and sung many beautiful hymns, but this particular one has always found a way to resonate with me the most: *"...and, He walks with me, and, He talks with me, and He tells me that I am His own, and the joy we share as we tarry there none other has ever known...!"* I've read many powerful homiletic sermons, and I have also written a few throughout my years of seminary studies, such as, ". . . Christ was destined. . . destined to hang on the cross for you and me. Christ suffered many trials and became the *Sacrificial Lamb* upon whose head heaped all the sins of the world!" Yes, Christ was destined. His destiny was given to Him by the Father, and without "fuss or fight," Jesus prayed His way through all trepidations. Strengthened by heavenly angels that ministered to His every need, through it all, Jesus Christ emerged victorious! Christ was anointed to do all that the Father called Him to do and to say.

CHAPTER 1

. . . .

"Don't Be a Gopher"

It has not always been a beautiful story; it's been a journey! Grandmother used to say, "Precious Chi'le, in this life you will face many ups and downs, hills and valleys, just don't be a gopher," meaning, "Don't 'go fer' anything and everything! I used to laugh, but her words still ring true. Born and raised in Southern Florida, in my adolescent, preteen days, I remembered just being a child having fun playing in the rain and mud, climbing and picking oranges and huge lemons from our backyard trees with no care in the world; so innocent in "heart and spirit" — just happy!

At a very young age, I dedicated my life to the Lord, and, as a PK, the majority of my upbringing, environment, and participation with others centered around family, school and church. In fact, this may sound a little strange to some, but I grew up not really knowing what a movie theater or skating rink looked like on the inside because my mother always tried to protect us. She did allow my brothers to go at times, but not me. Even my school friends knew that my mother did not play the radio, and still doesn't to this day (lol)! It did not bother me too much. In fact, I was okay with it because I spent a good portion of my time singing, feeding, distributing clothes to the homeless and participating in street evangelistic ministries on Saturday mornings, along with other home and church activities. I knew at a young age, I had a gift of healing through singing and a genuine, caring heart for people; so, I wanted to be around like minds. I am a lover of music and life. I love being happy and love seeing people happy.

Also, Mother never allowed me to spend a single night out from our home nor attend parties, that's something we as a family just didn't do. As I entered my first teenage years, she began to loosen her "tight grip" on me (chuckles). She started giving me permission to stay over at a certain friend's home, whom we knew well. I was often called her protégé in singing. She could sing so well —I mean she really sang! I had fun traveling and being around her, but then things began to take a turn.

One weekend I spent at her house, surprisingly and unwantedly (I didn't see it coming), one of her brothers took advantage of me. It shocked the hell out of me! I considered him as one of my own brothers. I cried silently, for at that very moment, my innocent spirit was being taken away . . . my world turned upside down . . . and sleep wouldn't come! The next day I awoke feeling vulnerable, embarrassed within, scared, used, and every ugly and detestable word I could think of. Still crying within and repeatedly saying in my head: "I lost my virginity!! And, I lost my virginity in a place that was supposed to be a safe haven."

Although it didn't feel good, and very inexperienced, I had just encountered sex for the very first time. It made me begin questioning myself: why didn't I have the guts to get up and walk away. . . ? Why is this happening to me? What did I do wrong? Who am I going to tell...I know that I'm a good-girl? The truth is, I did not know how to react in that unthinkable moment, I was still young - both in mind and body.

Then, unwantedly, it happened again: the next time, a few weeks later, I spent a night there and the other brother took advantage of me. I tried fighting him off without making a sound and, later, the burden of not saying anything weighed heavily upon me. Again, I felt I couldn't tell anyone, let alone the parents that their sons had taken advantage of me. And I could not bear the thought of telling my mother because of the absolute pain and disappointment it would cause her and my family. Besides, I was afraid everyone would think that I was the bad one.

There were a lot of positive experiences in hanging with my friend: I got to travel, eat at the best restaurants, wear shoes and clothes from top brands, and learn much about church music etiquette. However, no one knew how deeply I was hurting — how I felt like dying. A silent sadness rested on me, for I had begun to not like myself, and insecurities began to know my name. Unknown to her, there were a lot of pros and cons to our friendship. The betrayal I experienced and allowed to be put on my innocent spirit did NOT feel good; I had allowed someone to impose their dysfunction on me. And it changed my life; I tried my hardest to put it all in the far, far back corners of my mind. I was too young to experience such a thing!

My singing gift was apparent at an early age, I enjoyed singing, for to me, singing is like precious life itself, a sanctuary, however, it was often overshadowed and smothered because of jealousy and favoritism shown to others. I believe this was done to impress some leaders by choosing specific children for roles and solos over other gifted and anointed ones like myself. I began to feel a little insecure when anything became available, such as leading songs or participating on a greater level, because the same kids were always chosen, leaving the rest to be let down and play somewhat of "second fiddle." In some cases, it was hurtful! In my discouragement another part of me began to shut down, and repeatedly, I thought to myself: *only if they knew what happened to me, maybe, just maybe, things would be different!*

Mother did not know anything about the sexual abuse . . . and I was angry at her for NOT knowing! 'How could she allow this to happen to me?' I knew she knew nothing of it, for I never told her, so, she never had the opportunity to step in and protect me. (Mom and Grandmother were loving protectors). Hurting alone, all I could think of was the entire devastation it would cause my name, my family and my church.

That little "joyous personality" of a girl - full of life - had become fragilely devastated and forced into a shell of taunted secrecy. Not only could she not tell, who could she tell? Her only escape was to put it all on the "back burner" and continue with life. "Out of sight, out of mind," she simply moved on through life, trying not to think about it!

CHAPTER 2

"Just Plain Stupid – Naïve"

Still, in my early teens, I was extremely close to the young lady. I trusted her. I believed her; she had such a way of persuasion about her. I remember us being in a certain chain store shopping, when she gave her purse to me to "just carry" . . . or so I thought! I had no money with me because normally, she offered to pay for everything when we were together. I was on one aisle, and she was on another, when she asked me to come to her.

Then to my surprise, she took a piece of merchandise and placed it in the purse that I was carrying, her purse! (There I was being a 'gopher and naïve' again!) Instantly, I remembered the integrity and honesty instilled in both of us and became so embarrassed! However, she certainly disregarded that training at that moment! My mom was a single mother who made sure her children knew not to steal anything, always saying, "If you don't have enough money to pay for it, then you don't need it right now."

That was the philosophy preached in our household. So, when she stuffed that merchandise into the purse, I got so scared! I just knew someone was watching . . . just knew it! Nervously, I continued walking around the store for a bit more with her and as we were just about to exit, she walked out ahead of me, heading straight for the car. "Ma'am, ma'am!" It was the voice of the store's security officer behind me stopping me in my tracks . . . and the fear of my mom swept over me! I just knew I was dead! The fear of the Lord should have come over me first, but it was the fear of Mom (lol), then that of the Lord. *I'm going to jail!* was my third thought, as the guard grabbed me by my arm, instructing me to follow him. Tears upon tears started flowing at the thought of jail time!

As we walked into a security room housing their control cameras, he asked, "Uh, do you have something in your purse?" I hesitated for a few minutes, but I could not lie. . . I knew that he must have seen us . . . *Yeah, he saw us,* I thought. I mean I could not utter a word. "Well here, let me show you on the cameras," he offered.

Then I managed to say loudly, "It's not my purse, it's her purse!"

"Yes, but you have the purse; the merchandise is on you," he said.

Feeling helpless and scared, I began pleading, "No, you need to call her back in here. Tell her to come back in here!" "Uh, no, ma'am, we need to call your parents," he said.

With that, I immediately began telling him who her parents were. He was shocked! He repeated her father's name and other details. . . just to be sure we were referring to the same family. While still detained, sitting in that chair, with the crime still on me, I kept trying to convince him to go out to the car and get her, which he finally did. When he brought her in, the look she gave me was as if I had just "thrown her under the bus."

With mercy and grace, we heard him say while he was looking at the other young lady, "Because I know your parents, we're going to let this slide." Now, one side of me was happy to not be charged for a crime that I did not commit, but the other side of me was a little perplexed at the security officer's decision.

I realized at that moment that the only reason I got off was because of my association with her and her parents. Now, that taught me a valuable lesson at that age about the power of one's name, whether good or bad.

Later that day, when I told my mother about the mishap, I got a butt whipping that was 'out of this world'! To add to my punishment, I was not allowed to go over to my friend's for quite some time. While one side of me was happy, the other side longed for freedom. Moreover, Mom's punishment was very okay with me, I was safe.

What was imposed on me was not funny, not by any means! The childhood trauma caused me to begin exhibiting negative behavior and to not walk in my true identity. Though I was learning my identity, I did not demand others to acknowledge it. This is my first time ever talking about it after all these years. I had to learn to forgive myself, and forgive those who took advantage of my innocence . . . of me being so gullible and naïve. . . being a 'gopher.' I was hurt then on many levels, but, at this point in my healing, I can write this book —no longer a slave to the past. "Continue loving people. . . and forgive," I would often remind myself.

Today, it is important, DIVA, that no matter what is imposed on you in life— even in your darkest hour, your deepest moments of hurt —you can still somehow pull out genuine, godly love and extend grace to others. Though tough times may discourage you, affirm yourself and declare, "I am created for something better and greater . . . and I have got to show people love genuinely, because I know there's someone out there whose life is destined to change through God's love." Just don't be a gopher!

CHAPTER 3

"I'm Carrying Something"

Because of the dreams and premonitions that I was experiencing at a young age, I would sit in my high school classroom at my desk, daydreaming about singing and sometimes cry right there, thinking: "I know I should be out there serving and singing to someone with God's care and love." I didn't want to attend school, I just wanted to sing all day long.

It was in the chorus room where I most felt God's presence while at school. There was this young lady who was also in my music class who could sing well, too; she led basically all the songs we learned to sing. I thought to myself: *Here we go again.* There was no escaping the favoritism. Repeatedly, I asked myself, "Where do I fit in? How relevant am I?" I began to become introverted, although I'm not an introvert, I'm an extrovert, and full of life. Having to deal with favoritism caused me to become quiet and shy at times. Although I was always aware that I am a "smart cookie," I began feeling then as if my voice did not matter.

Nevertheless (sadly to say), I'll never forget that our chorus teacher used to ignore students' hands as they shot up (to volunteer), with a look on his face that often confirmed my assumptions: "Sorry, but you're not popular or influential enough to get a lead." It was as if he did not trust other students' abilities. As I matured, I began to realize what was really going on: I wasn't being chosen for a lead part because I lacked any skill or talent; people simply did not know what I was carrying, or just maybe they did. But I knew . . . and it was up to God to reveal my abilities in His timing!

As God allowed, and as I began to embrace my calling, doors began opening. No longer would I follow behind anyone's shadow, I was going to show up regardless. And the more I welcomed and embraced my gifts, the more they were revealed to others . . . my gifts made room for me! I never auditioned for any of the lead positions, any groups, or anything that I eventually participated in. I had begun to direct local church choirs, lend my voice to Prison Ministry outreach, and a plethora of other ministry and community activities. Being overlooked was unfortunate, but definitely a part of my destiny to help me grow into who I was becoming.

CHAPTER 4

· ·

"Blossoming Into..."

Entering my 12th grade year, I moved to Tyler, Texas, to live with an aunt and her husband. That's where I met Mrs. Coffee, my distinguished English teacher standing 5'2", very high arched eyebrows – her strong features resembled that of the renowned charismatic actress, Ms. Eartha Kitt. I remember her saying to me my first week in a very professional and astute manner: "Yes, yes, my dear, you're going to change many lives, you are a very beautiful and talented young lady, but you'd better know English, and you'd better pass my English class," while chuckling, classy, professional and serious all at the same time (lol). "How could you be a great singer if you don't know diction my dear?" She stayed on me every chance she could get, always reminding me: "There's so much in you." Yes, she had begun to really build me up, and this made a huge impact on my life because she pushed me to never settle.

After graduating high school and entering college in South Miami, I really wanted to make a stance for myself: I yearned to prove something not to anyone else, but to myself. Because of my involvement in campus music (Music Theory as my major study), and heavy involvement with the campus gospel choir, an opportunity came to me to perform for one of our student body events. So, with me as lead singer, I formed a group called "The Sequences." Two of us were from the same hometown and high school, and others we met while in college. We became close friends, like family (Hey ladies!). We cherished that opportunity to open up for an American R&B and electro-funk group that gained fame in the '80s, nationally and internationally, who remain very popular today. We were so stoked! (lol)

I was determined to perform: "This is my chance, this is a bigger arena," I told myself. Never will I forget the song we sang, *"Can't Go on Without You."* I was so proud of us! We received standing ovations before, during and after our performance. The emcee said, "I have to introduce the group to your peers and staff, what is your name?"

I replied, "LaDonna Michellé."

It felt like the beginning of a beautiful journey. When the emcee asked where I was from, I replied, "Tyler, Texas," which people from my hometown got a little upset about. "Why didn't you give hometown recognition?" they had asked. But I was thinking, *Well, that's where I came from to come here,* not aware, subconsciously, that I was still running from my past, from what had been imposed on me.

CHAPTER 5

....

"*Protection*"

As I tried to embrace my destiny fully there were still distracting thoughts: I wasn't great enough; or didn't know enough; or my opinion was of no value, that it didn't matter. And at times, circumstances and environments contradicted who I was *called* to be.

One such contradiction came while in college: I was at this well-known South Miami club, and I had had a few drinks. (That's when I tried 'social drinking' - wine for the very first time . . . and a time when I tried pulling away from the stigma of being a PK). While seated at the bar, watching people on the dance floor, with the room kind of smoky, I looked up, thinking I saw my mother walking across the dance floor. I said to myself: "Now, I know my momma, 'Pastor G' is not up in here!" So, I took a sip of my glass of wine again, peering again and thinking for sure that my mother walked across that floor.

A few minutes later, I could hear a voice in my head (in my spirit), say: "You need to leave." There I was trying to ignore the voice . . . and sat there . . . sipping on my drink some more, when suddenly the voice said again: "You need to leave." It got stronger, and louder, like an audible voice: "You need to leave NOW!" It scared me, and a few seconds later I grabbed my purse and got out of there, got in my car, backed out to start toward the expressway . . . no sooner than I was ready to take off, there was a mass shooting in the club! Terrified, I drove down the road with my hands shaking.

"Oh my God!" All I could say, repeatedly, was "Forgive me, Lord . . . Thank You, Lord! Thank You, Lord!"—driving and crying, just trying to get back to my dorm!

The next day my mother called and said to me: "I don't know where you were last night, but I couldn't rest. God's protection is all around you. I don't care what you do, where you go, you can't get away from prayer."

Then there was another time, when I accepted a private invitation to a house party at a mansion of a well-known rap producer (who is still alive today). I decided to not go alone and took my friend girls with me. We mingled around at first and then found ourselves a sitting area, just laughing and talking. I got up and went to the bar to get a glass of wine, and while standing there waiting for my drink, one of the rap producer's security guards approached the counter. He waited a few seconds then said, "Hi, Queen."

I said, "Hi" and then flipped my head back around (my hair cut was too short to sling my hair. . .lol).

When I was about to pick up my glass I heard again: "Queen."

I replied, "Yes." . . . thinking, *He's getting ready to hit on me . . . don't pay him any attention, shut up, shun him away.*

But then he said, "You know what, Queen? You don't belong here."

Those words shocked me . . . with somewhat of a guilty and embarrassing attitude, I said: "Excuse you . . .?!"

He continued: "You're out of place. There's something different about you; you don't belong here."

To my surprise, that resonated with me more than I had realized: someone who did not even know me saw more about me than I felt about myself at that moment. Even then, the angels of reminder and protection were with me!

I was reminded again of the level of greatness in me, that I was special (which I knew, though I didn't feel like it at that moment because of my earlier experiences in life). That man's words spoke directly to my spirit. Picking up my glass, I quickly said, "Have a great night" and walked back over to my friends. I sat there, staring into space for a few minutes, silently.

One of them asked, "Donna, what's wrong with you?"

I quickly replied, "Oh no, I'm good. I'm good."

"Are you having a good time?" she continued.

I insisted, "Yes. I'm having a good time."

After sitting for a couple more minutes, but restlessly, I finally uttered: "Umm, I'm getting ready to go . . . I'm not feeling too well. If y'all need me to come back and pick y'all up . . ."

I was cut off in mid-sentence: "No, we came with you," one said, "we're all leaving together."

So, all of us left together. As I drove, still remaining silent, I pondered to myself: *I can't run away from my giftings and callings, just can't. But how do I get over what was imposed on me?*

There was yet another situation in college, how I really came to know I was called by God. I once met this guy and there was little to somewhat of an attraction, only because I loved to dance, and he was a great dancer. Like many men back then, he wore a

Jheri curl (not sure what I was thinking right there!
. . . lol).

One evening we went dancing, and then out to
eat, ending up at his apartment. We both fell asleep.
In the middle of the night, I felt as if someone pushed
or jerked me and turning in my sleep to look, I saw
these black *things* flying over my head. (You know
how you're in a dream, and you can't move and can't
say anything, but you could see? That's how I felt!)
They kept flying over me and repeating, "Say, you
don't love Jesus, Say you don't love Jesus." I squirmed
and squirmed, tried to move, tried my best to speak .
. . when suddenly a massive image appeared in their
midst and said with a heavier voice than theirs: "Say,
you don't love Jesus, Say you don't love Jesus."

I squirmed again vigorously and suddenly belted
out: "I love Jesus. I love Jesus. I love Jesus!" The huge
one did not move or even flinch, and I thought:
Maybe he didn't hear me —though I just knew I was
yelling! Although I could not see them anymore, I
could feel their evil presence still there. So, I could
not sleep... and could not wait until daylight to come!

Instead of sleeping, I remembered my upbringing
and began praying . . . and as soon as a little daylight
broke, I nudged him and said: "I want to go back to
my dorm." He got up and took me back.

Later that morning, even before I could call my
mother to tell her about the dream, she called me

(prayer warrior and intercessor that she is), saying: "Michellé, the power of the Holy Spirit is on you, you cannot run. You weren't in the dorm last night. I couldn't rest. I don't know where you were, but you cannot run from the power of the Holy Ghost. You cannot run from the Lord." That incident made me a believer once again! I was called. I am different. I am set aside for a special work.

Yet again, I had escaped the trap of the little road I was trying to go down, of *trying to fit in*. I could only go but so far because of my mother's and grandmother's prayers and the Bible; they were like a yoke around my neck, keeping me from straying off course. You might say that I was in the wrong place at the right time to learn those lessons . . . just wish I had been obedient to my calling, fully. Which brings me to this point: trying to fit in only moves you further away from your true calling. Your life's journey is already set for you, take courage and walk in it. You are already predestined. We are already predestined. We must seek out our purpose, our destiny, and walk in it. That's it!

CHAPTER 6

"I See You..."

I was developing into a young lady with nice curvy legs, a lovely spirit, and personality, *but* it was how I treated others that made me feel beautiful. Even now. People were always saying that there is a *glow* about me, but, admittedly, there were still certain lessons I had not yet learned.

Some folks can tell when you're innocent; they can tell if you're inexperienced, even those in the religious sector. Before becoming "church people" or members, some of them were "street people."

My tender years of development had taught me when something didn't feel right. Having been manipulated into prior compromising situations, I began to recognize when a conversation, an advance or touch was not appropriate. And that kind of behavior always threw me into an introverted state where I could not really express my uniqueness nor my genuine and respectful love for others —without fear of being taken advantage of! Some would think that I was easy, especially if I smiled and or talked friendly.

Some would try to size me up, until I took a firm stance and refused even to converse with them. I walked away and just simply said "No" if I felt unsafe. Sometimes I had to remind them (and even remind myself) that I had given my life to the Lord . . . and even ask: "Do you know who my mother is?" Mother had worked for the state government in our hometown, as well as an RN; she knew a lot of people.

Others knew her from our community involvement and church connections as well. So, I'd threaten to tell my mother if I felt they used inappropriate gestures towards me. They would say, "We don't want no trouble from 'Pastor G'!" or "You don't have to mention her name . . . we don't want any trouble from her."

They even said, "Oh, I know your people; you come from good stock." Most people knew that, but they still didn't know my story. Now, I was not a "goody two-shoes" living with unhealed trauma, insecurities and inner hurt at a young age, I also became a single mother of two in my twenties (I'm proud of my children - hey kids, mommy loves you!). Nonetheless, I continued doing what I loved most, singing. Traveling and singing with others . . . I saw a lot "trying to fit in" . . . "*I knew we all were better than what I was seeing, but on the other hand, how else would people know I could sing if I didn't try to 'fit in the in crowd'?*" I felt stuck. To be 100% honest, it still happens today for so many; almost as if one has to "sell your soul," meaning participate in compromising situations to get to "the top."

That stuff is done in and on all levels, but I never could . . . just couldn't . . . and won't. I'd ask, "*God, how else would people know that I'm called?*" So, I had to grow and learn; seek to be safe and allow the Lord to lead and guide me. My mother would always say: "Michellé, at God's appointed time, *all* your gifts will make room for you - don't try to fit in, just be watchful and prayerful and obedient," a wholesome phrase she still speaks. Everything that I dealt with at that point had become a pivotal point in my life journey: I prayed, "*Lord, I don't want to be looked at as a sex object, a 'go fer', naïve or gullible or anything that You did not called me to be!*" DIVA, never seek to be popular - more specifically, never seek to be popular especially if it means having to compromise who you are *called* to be. God has already chosen and prepared your platform and your audience . . . you are not meant to fit in. You are one-of-a-kind!

CHAPTER 7

"Searching for True Calling and Purpose – Searching for Me"

When you allow unspoken or suppressed experiences to go unhealed and left in the dark as if they do not exist, you begin to question yourself: *"If I'm so destined, why is this happening to me?"* or *"God, don't you see me - help me? You made me; You predestined me for greatness. You predestined me for love, joy, happiness, and peace, but why is this happening to me? In some likeness, I can identify with (Judges 6:13 -16 NIV)"* My questions finally led to this one important question: *"LaDonna, do you really know who you are?"* I would have resisted all that was imposed on me, if I had fully known *me*. In order to answer those life-altering questions, I had to do some deep soul searching. In my late twenties, I literally moved from one state to another and, only later, realized a part of me was running *from* what had occurred . . . the other part was running *to* discover who I was *called* to be.

I wanted to know my real destiny. What exactly had God created me for? Had I allowed myself to be used, to be taken advantage by others? It bothered me that I was so naïve . . . "green." Who was to blame, really? The growing anguish within became a "fire" forcing me to rediscover myself, and once I did, I knew without a doubt that there was greater within. I just had to figure out how to rise from beneath those "dark shadows" and "ashes" to reveal my gifts, talents, joy, godly love!

After relocating, a Mega Church I started attending became my spiritual home and I quickly became involved in its music ministry, at times leading praise and worship and directing a 200/250 - voice women's choir. A few years later, I became part of its ministerial alliance, in which I remain active. My gifts were being discovered by a plethora of platforms and I was beginning to glow again! But, at times, the quiet moments found me hurting myself by repeating negative thoughts in my mind instead of addressing them - the mind is certainly a battlefield.

Knowing their root cause and who would be damaged, I still kept the past trauma all to myself.

Occasionally throughout the years, I remained in contact with the sisters and certain members of my abusers' family. We were all friends. Although we grew up together, the families knew nothing about the abuse. Despite that, I have always known greatness lies within me, and I want it to matter.

And it does matter! I am destined to share God's love, joy, gifts and talents with the world. It was time to be relevant, time to walk in my own footsteps, not in anyone's shadow. Once breaking free, I felt good, really good, as if on top of the world! "This joy that I have, the world didn't give it to me . . .." I was truly in a joyful place.

CHAPTER 8

"Marriage: Pray First ... Don't Rush In!"

Approaching my 30's, I was ready to settle down and get married; and a few years later, I did! I was happy and proud of my new blended family. Wait one second, let me talk about this handsome southern man! I met my ex-husband 21 years ago on a rainy Saturday morning in April. We started talking on the phone by me accidentally mis-dialing my hairdresser's number. But what a pleasant conversation we had! From that day on, he called me every day, sometimes three and four times a day . . . and his attention and care towards me made an impression on me. It took us nearly three months before meeting face-to-face, when he accepted my invitation to meet me at my church. Talking about nice looking! He had a clean-shaven head, big, wide smile, with bright teeth, pecan tan complexion, 50 athletic cut, 18 1/2" neck and a 36/38" waist. Oh, my, my . . .! We started attending church together on a regular basis and it felt like the beginning of a new and destined journey, as we began blending our families together. By that time, I thought I was doing everything right that I needed to do towards building a great relationship. It felt right!

Soon, everything went so quickly, our relationship skyrocketed! One of the reasons we decided to marry so soon, we discovered we were with child and went straight to the courthouse and got married! Not really getting to know one another deeper or allowing our friendship to grow was the beginning of a mistake.

Our first years as a newly married couple were fun and amazing, being young and happy, raising children, and both with good jobs. We built our first home from the ground up. We traveled everywhere did. . . everything a normal family does. Everything was beautiful! In the words of R&B sensation Keith Sweat, let's "make it last forever," and stay married for decades - "until death do us part." My desire was to only marry once.

The next few years were okay as we began to settle down. Like all new families, we began experiencing challenges: my ex-husband had a terrible trucking accident, suffering major injury to his arm. Our finances then took a huge plunge, one mishap after another! Our new family was beginning to fall apart and after the ninth year, or so, separation. Although we felt that we loved each other, we weren't *in love* with one another. There wasn't enough foundation there to hold the union together. We grew apart emotionally . . . and finally divorced.

Growing up, I would more often hear church mother's and others say, "Hunny, fight for your marriage, it's not all that bad. Stay in the marriage even if it's not working out, you'll get used to it - it all will work out in the end." I used to believe that, but I don't fully embrace that concept any longer. Don't get me wrong, fight to a certain extent. Fight until you can't fight anymore or bargain with the trauma of it all. . . but, if it's not working, it's not working. For many years, I carried guilt regarding my separation and failed marriage.

But know this, even when a marriage becomes rocky or fails, never feel guilty or blame anyone, not even yourself. From the very beginning, when a relationship or marriage is unequally yoked, that's a recipe for failure. We both admit now that we should have done it right from the very beginning: prayer, biblical principles and premarital counseling. Marriage is a holy institution created by God and intended to be a lifelong commitment. When you step in and take charge without praying, without *fully* applying God's Word regarding marriage or even consideration of it, there is bound to be failure. Although your intentions for one another may be in the right places in the beginning, oftentimes, we still miss the mark. Note this: my ex-husband is a God-fearing man and a very good father, and to this day, we are still parental friends, sharing our parental duties peacefully.

Remember, the heart can deceive . . . wise counsel is important, especially when you are in a vulnerable state of mind. This is the wisest of counsel:

*"Trust God from the bottom of your heart; don't try to figure out everything on your own. Listen for God's voice in everything you do, everywher*e you go; he's the one who will keep you on track. Don't assume that you know it all"* (Proverbs 3:5-6 MSG).

CHAPTER 9

. . . .

"Process & Timing"

To have that real gift of love, joy, and happiness, I had to wait on God's timing. Nothing can be forced; it is a process. Neither is it always a "feel good" time, because sometimes you fall into a hurtful and lonely place in your mind, the enemy working on your self-esteem, pushing you to try to please your flesh and move before time. You even at times are doubting the Father, what He has said about you.

I had to learn that if I am going to do this thing the right way, to walk in His footsteps toward destiny, I must walk in integrity and wait on Him and do what He wants done in my life. Were it not for God's grace and mercy, I would miss His perfect timing. It's vitally important to wait on God's timing, for if you lose your divine purpose, you lose everything.

Every prayer you've prayed to the Lord, whenever you prayed it, He will bring you through at an appointed time. Just apply the Word: *"Wait on the Lord; Be of good courage, And He shall strengthen your heart; Wait, I say, on the Lord!" (Psalm 27:14 NKJV).* In many circumstances, it will not be easy, but it is very necessary.

Every moment, every situation in life is precious; and every battle in life is important, even those ugly, ugly moments. Each situation you experience is for the upbuilding of your character, for your growth and continual preparation on life's journey. God's timing is impeccable. Walk in His truth. Live in His truth. God gives you *grace* to understand . . . to grow . . . to keep moving forward and to love. So, continuously push yourself to love no matter what you have experienced . . . push yourself to forgive and to love people, unconditionally. I am glad that the Lord showered me with His gift of love, grace, and forgiveness. Do your part, and He'll do the rest. Remember...you are *becoming.*

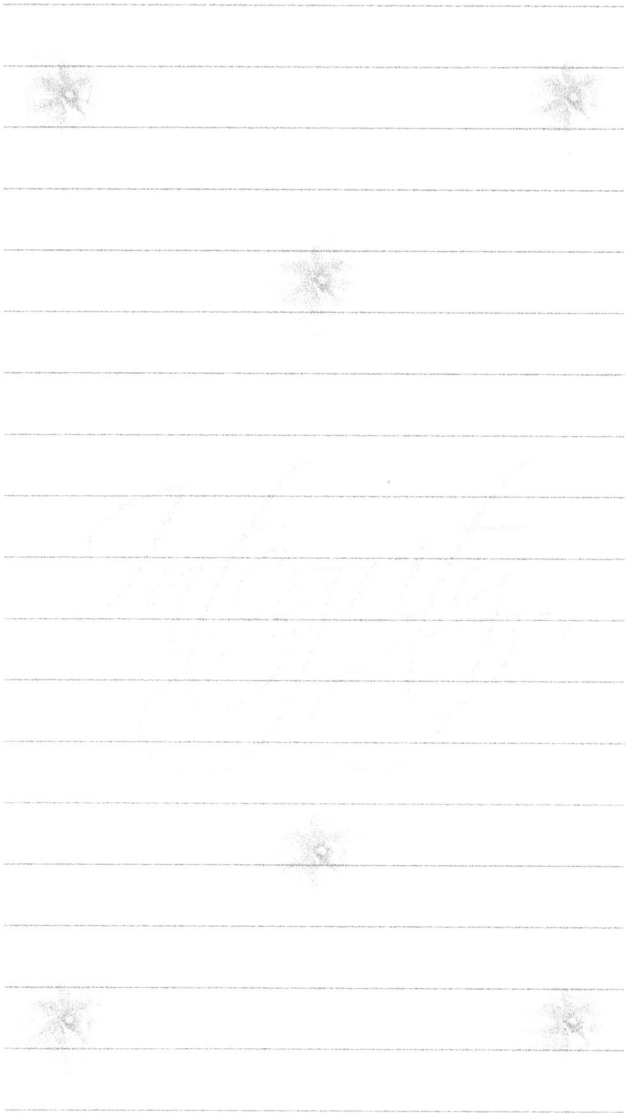

CHAPTER 10

"Know Your Worth ... Don't Get Stuck"

Oftentimes knowing your worth is revealed in and through relationships, whether they are every day, romantic, or spiritual ones. More often, some people may choose to love you based on the amount of things and love you can give to them.

Years later, I was in a very happy place again, loving my life, my work, social life, traveling extensively, and all life entailed. One day something happened: this gentleman introduced himself to me via social media. He started "liking" all my photos and leaving comments openly. And then out of the blue, he in-boxed me: "Hi, beautiful. Every time I see your post, they're so life-changing."

"Hi, thank you," I replied, "Is this concerning business?

He answered, "No, I just want to get to know you."

I pointed out to him that, "I don't do in-box messaging unless it's business."

However, he persisted: "I would like to get to know you."

Normally, I do not accept in-box conversations from men unless it is strictly business, my company's practice that I still hold firm today. I asked once more: "Is this in reference to business? If not, I'm going to delete you."

"Why would you delete me?" he said. "I know I could love you if you gave me a chance."

I thought to myself and then questioned him: "Love me? You don't even know me!" Yet it intrigued me that he said *love.* So, the next time he in-boxed me a few days later, right away I said, "I'm going to delete you."

Then he stated, "Wait, wait don't delete me, please! Why would you push away what *God* sent to you?"

Those very words right there stopped me in my tracks, they caught my attention and reminded me of his use of the word *love* the other day. Now he was asking, "Why would I push away what God sent to me?" And then it struck me: *LaDonna, am I really pushing away a gift from God?* I became a little curious, and so my work focus was disrupted.

After we engaged in a more extended conversation, he immediately sent over all his telephone numbers, which I let sit in my in-box for nearly two weeks. I was a little hesitant, thinking to myself, a man with all those phone numbers was certainly up to something strange. Against my better judgment, I finally called him.

He answered with "Hi beautiful, oh my God, it's about time, Queen . . ."

"Hi there," I said, and our conversation started.

He was polite, and he had a smooth, but rugged-toned voice, seemed business-oriented and caring, not to mention, looking at his social media profile picture, he was very handsome... traits a woman certainly would admire. I did. I even nicknamed him "Beautiful Ears," for he seemed to have a way of listening to me. We would talk, text and video chat several times a day, I was beginning to really like him. I could tell that his feelings were growing for me as well.

It was at a nice restaurant that we first met face-to-face. Falling deeper for him, one day, I just picked up the phone and called him, saying, "Hey, I'm on your side of town having lunch."

Hastily - quite energetically - he asked, "Well, where are you beautiful?"

I told him, and he said that he was on his way and hung up the phone immediately. I thought to myself:

This man does not even know if I'm with somebody or not. Several minutes later, when he walked through those restaurant doors, I knew exactly that it was him. He was wearing a cream fedora hat, a nicely shaven beard, was handsome and had a magnetic vibe like none other. I thought, *Oh, my gosh - that's the one for me!* I stood up to shake his hand, but he went straight for a hug. Boy, do I remember the way he hugged me . . . circling within my jacket and raising his hand up my back. I had never been touched like that! There was an instant electrifying connection between the two of us.

We sat down, he had so much energy, very charismatic.

"Oh my God, your pictures don't do you any justice, you're so beautiful?" he declared.

"Well, I don't know about that... and you're handsome," I replied with a gentle smile.

That is how it all began! I began to repeatedly say in my head, "Lord, let this be the one! Let him be the truth! If not, please get me out of this" – but could not deny the attraction between us. After eating, as I walked outside, he pulled up to the curb in his pearl white 750i, got out, and opened the passenger door for me. There was a feeling deep down inside of me really hoping and praying that he was indeed the one...too seasoned in age for tricks and games.

As I proceeded to get in the car, I heard an elderly lady nearby say, "Happy Easter, you look beautiful."

I turned to say, "Thank you Mother," while thinking to myself: *Lord, I hope she's praying for me . . .* (lol).

We got in the car, and as I reached for my seat belt, he said, "Please don't do that," and then he reached over and buckled me in.

Humm, a perfect gentleman, I thought. It all felt so natural.

He asked if he could stop by a nearby chain store to shop for white pillows. I said, "Yes." And as we entered the store, people looked admiringly at us as if we were this "star couple." He felt right to me. I went searching on one side of the aisle, while he on the other.

"Hey babe!" he said - which got my attention . . . again, it felt natural. By now I was praying that this time of being in a relationship, it was *real*. "Do you see anything?" he asked.

I answered, "No." So, we left and walked into the next chain store and went straight back to the pillows. "Oh, my gosh!" I exclaimed, which got his attention.

He replied, "What baby?"

(I paused . . . he'd said *baby* again; something I wanted and desired to hear). It felt honest and genuine and I happily responded: "I found the perfect pillows."

He walked around to me and said, "Baby, you like those?"

I said, "Yes, I love them." They were beautiful, large, white, faux fur throw pillows –huge ones!

He started pulling them off the shelf hastily, and I managed to grab two to carry. He said, "Come on, baby, let's go," and we walked to the register and purchased them all.

As we walked back to his car, he looked thoughtfully at me and said, "Babe, you're a good woman."

And I responded with, "Well, yeah."

After tucking the pillows in the trunk, he opened my door, put my seatbelt over me, then off we drove. "Let me drop these off to my house first," he announced more than asked. *Oh, God!* I cringed; I knew that if we went to his house, that was it! But I had grown and matured emotionally and spiritually by leaps and bounds, I just knew that I wasn't going to cave in that easily, I just knew it.

The next morning, shamefully waking up in his arms, I felt convicted on many levels. . . and not to mention, it was Easter Sunday.

My family's tradition, growing up, was to rise early, get ready for breakfast, iron each other's clothes, make long-distance calls to other families, and then get ready for church. We went to church as a family unit. I felt bad that Sunday! –that was my first-time missing Easter service in years! I was torn.

As we stayed in, he began calling his family members. I was excited to see that he was a family man, too, but I still felt utterly convicted. I thought to myself, *Girl, what are you doing? Get yourself together. This is not like you, this not you missing church services either*. He called later that day and said that he really missed me. Something inside of me missed him too, I longed for that. My thought was that he had finally found me, and I had opened up and accepted him in my life. Sharing several conversations became a daily routine. We both began to frequently use the words "I Love You," it felt right. We were doing a few things that new couples would do together.

We attended a particular meeting with a business colleague of his from Florida. I had arrived late at the designated restaurant. Noticing that I had entered, he announced, "There's Lady." After greeting him first (with a hug, of course), I then circled the entire table, shaking hands with the host and others before taking my seat. It was no shock to me that each man stood up out of respect as they greeted me, which he obviously had taken notice of because he leaned in towards me even more. I humbly relished their show of respect; it was especially pleasing to me that he had witnessed it. Throughout future outings and meetings, occasionally we would attend, he would notice that I received much respect.

Things were good, but I began sensing a hint of jealousy, manipulation and control coming from him. . .all the red flags! One evening, as we were dining and having a great time laughing and talking, he suddenly turned to me and said, "Hey Baby", with what seemed a seductive look on his face.

"Yes, what, Babe?" I asked.

Then taking a puff on his cigar, and looking straight at me again, he said: "You know what? You my b..." Those words that came out of his mouth - what he called me - put me in total disbelief! –and hurt to the core! It was most humiliating!

I have heard men and women both say that "b... . ." is *not* such a bad word, that it only means "you're my ride or die," but I am a respectable woman and - in my world - I have never been called that! Never! Granted he's 100x's more street smart than me. . . but in my world, I have never been called out of my name! (How can anyone justify equating a human being with a dog that keeps birthing puppies? That is the definition, right?) At that point, I knew for sure that this man was slowly showing disrespect for me. Things certainly did not start out that way . . . and after 3 years how he had switched up certainly had begun to confuse me.

Because of the love you have for someone, that person can hurt you, really hurt you. And here you come two or three days later forgiving them and taking them back! Even willing to accept breadcrumbing from them. There I was allowing his manipulative words and actions to overshadow my worth - just to show him unconditional love. I really was *in* love. I fell in love with him and he knew it. However, though he said he loved me - all the time - his actions and words did not always match. I felt his mounting disrespect . . . wondered too if he was hiding something. I was slowly losing my self-identity.

My mother would always pray for the two of us, but one day she asked me: "How much are you willing to lose of yourself to love him?" I told her that it was not like that . . .

To this she replied: "Obviously it is. I hear the hurt and pain of disappointment in your voice. He hurt you verbally by calling you out of your name, he's emotionally manipulative, and plays controlling mind games. He gets upset easily. You don't hear from him for a day or two, that's manipulation sweetie, open your eyes."

I had no proof but felt he was doing something with someone else. In fact, there were times when I would have visions or dreams . . . and begin crying because of them. Then I would encourage myself:

"Get a grip, Lady LaDonna!" "God, help me. Don't let me hurt anymore. Please reveal this man to me!"

The Lord was revealing to me, just as I had asked. I began seeing things I once overlooked. He would say things to me that I began noticing as "red flags" . . . when before, I used to think he could do no wrong. All at the same time, I was losing myself, my self-worth. Let me back up a little: God was revealing the truth to me loudly, but I was overlooking it because, selfishly, I wanted to make it work. I found myself praying: *Well, I do love him, and he says that he loves me deeply. If you love him, Lady, pray for him, pray him into the body of Christ.* So, there I was trying to rationalize and spiritualize how to stay connected together with this man.

Believing I heard God say that *If I let go of him, in less than six months He would give him back to me a changed man*, seemed assuring, but still, I was afraid of letting him go. Then the Lord spoke: "Let him go; he's not yours, he's Mine." Anything (or anyone) you put before the Lord is wrong . . . and God is a jealous God. He will separate you quickly, no matter how bad you want it, or how bad it hurts. Wishing and wanting to have your own way will have you scattered in your emotions. Girl, I am here to tell you, let go! Let God! "If that man is meant for you, after you let go, God will send him running back to you!" If not, keep it stepping. There's another one, only better next time! If you didn't know before, now you know: "soul-ties" are real!

Now I can say, I have climbed onto the other side of total healing, having let go. I no longer feel that tie or burden deep in my belly; it was either God or him . . . I chose God. And because I asked, it was God who gave me power to let him go –God did it! It is extremely important to stay in the will of the LORD. But, if you should find yourself out of His will, get back quickly! God's timing is perfect, and in His perfect timing, God will reveal all. Do not let anyone or anything distract you. In that past relationship, I "believed" - "Beautiful Ears" loved me too, but I knew God loved me more and my desire was (still is) for God above all else.

Things don't always work out the way you wish for, and even prayed...geesh, don't I know! This journey, this positive journey that I am now on has me moving forward in life on an accelerated, upward path with purpose and destiny. I *Know my Worth! I Embrace my Worth*! *I Walk in my Worth!* I cannot mess this up!

CHAPTER 11

"I Think I Can . . . Break Free"

Much of my journey reminds me of "The Little Engine That Could," saying, "I think I can. I think I can. I think I can." I think I can keep moving, I think I can get over the insecurities, doubts, fears, and the stigma of failed relationships. I think I can get out of the trapped cycles and find peace. First, I asked God for forgiveness. I must forgive myself and others in order to walk in self-love, self-value, self-confidence. Yes, I *know* I can! But then comes something that is stronger than that last situation or last test you went through, and it comes around again just to try you . . . to see if you're going to stick to your guns!

When you look for validation, or anything of that sort, from people rather than from the Lord and from within, you then get trapped in various toxic cycles or situations. Self-doubt sets in, you then begin to settle into mediocrity, and none of us are called to be mediocre. DIVA, you must have the will power - "guts"- to break through that mental battle! "How?" you may ask. You accomplish this by embracing a lifestyle of consistent prayer, by reading God's Word, and by being around motivated and strong-minded people who hold you accountable. "I Think I Can, I Know I Can, I Will and I Did."

There is a familiar saying: "When you wake up in the morning, fear wakes up at the same time." In other words, just as you're up and getting ready to start your day, believing it is going to be a great day, in walks fear and adversity trying to get your attention first. Disarm them both! Declare the Word over yourself: *"God has not given me the spirit of fear; but of power, and of love, and of a sound mind"* (II Timothy 1:7). You have the power and you have the authority to evict both villains. Use it, shut the door speedily! You have the mind of Christ . . . they have to flee.

CHAPTER 12

"Girl, You Got This!"

Rejection, fear, and operating in a lack of self-worth, or self-love, are all taunting and hurtful to one's purpose and journey. If it were left up to some individuals, we would certainly skip parts of our journey. Instead, we must learn to walk through the process, while understanding that we all have a destiny, a purpose; and each of us has a place on earth to help spread this knowledge –this truth.

D.I.V.A: There is much more to us than what society has coined for us: we are destined . . . we are integrity . . . we are victorious . . . we are anointed . . . and we are called! You and I are especially called to do something specific, for a specific group of people, for a specific time . . . called to all of that and much more! I had to realize this truth when it came to my calling and then declare, "Girl, I got this."

No matter what was imposed on me, no matter what I have gone through, my destiny has never changed. No matter what I have faced –no matter the circumstances– what matters is that it was all for the building up of who I was *called* and are *becoming* today, in this present world. I am not above going through anything, but I can truthfully declare again: if it had not been for the grace and the mercy of God, I would not have made it. God's grace is shining through my life; His grace is mine to be better . . . and His grace is mine to be empowered. I am not sorry, nor do I apologize or make excuses for my story.

Instead, my constant prayer is, *"LORD, forgive me for my unbelief and for the times that I did not stand in faith."* In victory and empowerment. . . is where I stand today! I Am Destined. I Am Integrity. I Am Victorious. I Am Anointed. That's who God *called* me to be, and MUCH more! And I have the will to love no matter what . . . for *I Am D.I.V.A.*

Let me encourage you: **you got this!** Do not be afraid to fully embrace your identity, love your identity and walk with confidence in it! God has already predestined you to become who you are becoming for His kingdom, His glory, and for His people in this time and space. Therefore, do not be afraid.

CHAPTER 13

"The Mess, The Miracle, The Manifestation"

When we were created, we were created in God's likeness, in His image. I am talking about God, the Creator of this world –All-Powerful, All-Knowing, Ever-Present and Pure above all!

In living our lives, though we are created purely for a purpose, we can get "beside ourselves," for the lack of understanding our purpose. Such lack leads us deep into our own thoughts, our own free will, ultimately pushing us onto a different road than that we were originally created for. Our "journey" then turns into our "mess" because we begin doing things on our own, implementing our vain and selfish thoughts, taking our eyes off our Maker.

Our flesh wants to enjoy things we think are good for us, not realizing we are totally off the path of our God-given purpose. Some may start allowing drinking, smoking, or any misuse of our bodies, our "temples of the Holy Spirit." As a result, we become double-minded and uncertain. God's Word states that a *double-minded man is unstable in all his [her] ways.* This then is downright confusion; it is debilitating, and, therefore, our only clarity will come from our original Creator, when we turn back and seek Him.

If you don't know what you're doing, pray to the Father. He loves to help. You'll get his help, and won't be condescended to when you ask for it. Ask boldly, believingly, without a second thought. People who "worry their prayers" are like wind-whipped waves. Don't think you're going to get anything from the Master that way, adrift at sea, keeping all your options open" (James 1:5-8 MSG).

When you've been pulled back into reality and say, "Okay, enough is enough!" no longer straddle the fence, no longer double minded, you've now set yourself on the road to recovery. Know from the very beginning, God knows you and loves you, unconditionally.

When I rededicated my life back to God, refocused and re-aligned myself, I began to regain stability in every aspect: my physical life, my finances, my mind, and my soul. Greater and better favor was thrust upon me, taking me to the next level!

When you are purposed and destined for something great – I do not care where you go, maybe even to "hell & back" it seems – you are still destined. You must fulfill your destiny and purpose, which you were predestined for before your birth.

Never would I have thought I would become the woman that I am today. It is manifesting even as I write . . . and writing and living without any fear. God told me to do this, and I am just being obedient. By being obedient, doors and blessings will open for you too because I am assigned to certain people, and certain people are assigned to me. So, I am glad that I went through the process of my mess. My mess led to my miracles! Now, manifestation is here, happening at this moment. And I do believe that God is pleased!

I have come to know truly that I am God's "biggest addiction"; He loves me no matter what! I know for a fact that He is rooting for me and for you. Even when you are down, He is rooting for you. When you are trying to get up and do not have much clarity, He is rooting for you. When you have become enlightened and begin walking in your destiny, He is rooting for you. He is a Friend of all friends.

Yes, I believe that I am His biggest "addiction" . . . the Word says, I am the *apple of His eye,*" meaning His *"teaching is as precious as your eyesight*

—*guard it!*" (Prov. 7:2 MSG) —meaning *He loves me unconditionally*, above all else. Now, we mustn't get it wrong: Even in our mess God still loves us, though He is disappointed. His love is unconditional, it overshadows all our messes, and the truth is that we can sing along with a friend of mine: *"I am a friend of God . . . He calls me 'friend'."*

I have disappointed Him throughout my life, and probably will disappoint Him again, though surely not on purpose . . . but I probably will. I am thankful for new mercies every day, thankful to know that if I make a mistake, I can repent before God, my Father . . . can go on with life knowing that His love for me has not changed. God will not stop loving me, and God will not stop loving you.

"Dear D.I.V.A."

"Everything that you've gone through in life, God uses it to help paint a picture of who you are to become! Now turn around and give it all back to Him for healing of the masses. If only I would have known *Me* in me! But, that's okay, I'm glad that I made it this far! Besides, our timing is not God's timing. Our calling is to know the "unknown ways of God's will" (see Ephesians 1:9). I believe more than often, our lives are disrupted, on purpose. It is for all kinds of *life* reasons. Moreover, we must be determined to seek our higher calling.

We all have become vulnerable in our lives; we all have gotten off the path when all sorts of things influence us: compliments, attention from a good-looking sexy man, good gestures, sweet nothings . . . overlooking all the warning signs - the "red flags," because he seems to know just what we need for that moment. Always guard your heart!

"Above all else, guard your heart, for everything you do flows from it. Keep your mouth free of perversity; keep corrupt talk far from your lips. Let your eyes look straight ahead; fix your gaze directly before you. Give careful thought to the paths for your feet and be steadfast in all your ways. Do not turn to the right or the left; keep your foot from evil" (Proverbs 4:23 NIV).

We don't have to choose to be deceived nor abused, whether it's mentally, emotionally or physically.

Although things may not be perfect in life, with the Lord's grace you can find your way back on the right track. So, I leave you with this: never allow anyone to measure you by their definition of validation of who you are and who you're destined to be. Your purpose and destiny are in God's Hands.

He knows your journey, already knew what it would take for you to become who you were created to be. God knows the very number of hairs on our head and He knows every thought before you can think it! He's the Orchestrator, knowing everything that we are going to do before we do it, all our choices. He is All-knowing!

I am so grateful that He allowed me to process through an ugly journey just to be on this side of *manifestation.* The Lord allowed me to get to know *me* before I could share with *you.* No matter if it is a friendship or relationship on a spiritual level or personal level, get to know yourself first. Once you do that, when people come into your life, you can accept or not accept them you will have strength to do one or the other. Remember, the only validation you need in life comes from above. Believe in yourself, love yourself, and love others.

When you find yourself on an unpleasant journey in life, ask God for the gift of His guidance. Ask Him for the accompanying gifts of forgiveness, grace, mercy, understanding, and ask for wisdom to get back to walking out your predestined journey.

If you have gleaned nothing else from what has been shared, please allow me now to offer this final insight. When you truly know who you are and whose you are – despite any past failures, any fears, despite what others have imposed on you, what others may have said to or about you or what you may have said to or about yourself; despite any insecurities or inadequacies, whatever has held you back from being the D.I.V.A. you are – YOU, dear woman, are more than enough. You, D.I.V.A., are destined for greater.

You, D.I.V.A., are destined. There is so much you have to offer . . . the world is waiting! And when you finally get to that place of destiny, that place that affirms and fortifies your purpose, I promise you: those who have been waiting –Oh, so long for you!

– will be overjoyed and may even ask, "What took you so long?" There is no one better at being you than you; no one who can do what you have been purposed to do better than you. The "blessing with your name on it" will be null and void if you choose to not accept the fact that you are, indeed, destined.

You, D.I.V.A., are integrity. Did you know, somebody's watching you? It may be your daughter or the little girl down the street. It could be the guy you thought never even noticed you. Maybe it is the superior on your job, wondering how you would fare if the right opportunity within the company presented itself to you. What do they see when they see you? Will it be a show for applause, or will it be your most authentic self of always endeavoring to do the right thing, regardless of whether someone notices? The latter is who you are capable of being; never let anyone tell you anything different.

You, D.I.V.A., are victorious. Just look at all the "mountains" you've climbed and "valleys" you've pressed your way through. Oh my, what a journey! Think of the times when you could have given up but something on the inside kept telling you to hang on in there. You did! And guess what? You're still here . . . still standing! You may have had to re-navigate your route but that is an insignificant factor, what matters is that you did not allow your detour to deliver defeat.

Even when it looks like you are down for the final count, you are victorious, dear D.I.V.A.

You, D.I.V.A., are anointed. Do not shy away, misconstrue, or misunderstand the word *anointed*. The church generally equates it to the laying on of hands with anointed *oil*. But know that with that, too, God has called and predestined you (each of us) with a purpose. I may not have what you have, and you may not have what I have; *anointed* simply means being specifically *called out* and *set apart* to walk into something unique and different from everyone else's gift. And don't get it twisted my D.I.V.A., anointing does not make one better than another.

There is no obstacle that could ever come your way that you cannot get over. Have you ever wondered why? Because you've endured enough. You've passed enough tests. You've cried enough tears. There is nothing left to do now but stand up straight, hold your head up high, square your shoulders, stick your chest out, and claim the blessings that have been waiting on you. The trials you have overcome produced an oil of resilience, ushering you right to where God would have you to be. What a feeling!

Go forward from this point on, D.I.V.A., with the full confidence that, beyond a shadow of doubt, you are destined, you are integrity, you are victorious, and you are anointed. The days of being anything less than either of these qualities are long gone. Go ahead, D.I.V.A... live your best life! And while you are at it, we will be right here rejoicing with you!

Love is the most important gift of all. And when you have the gift of genuine love, you will know exactly who you are and whose you are. I Am D.I.V.A. . . . a woman who's destined. . . a woman walking in integrity . . . a woman who's victorious . . . and a woman who's anointed. That is who God called me to be and MUCH more. God bless you beautiful Queen!

~ Lady LaDonna

Lady LaDonna

People would often ask me my name, and where I got that name from, or why I go by the name Lady LaDonna? I would get offended at times by all the questioning: my name is LaDonna, meaning "the lady," but I didn't always *understand* myself as such throughout my early years. So, I asked God, "God, why Lady LaDonna?"

He responded: "Because you're going to live up to that name in its entirety from now on. You have not been counted out." Yet I still did not fully understand.

Then one day, many years ago, a musician who was big in the gospel industry called me to do backstage management for a live taping with a Gospel Fest event in Atlanta. We had met previously at a larger VIP music workshop where musicians, gospel singers, and preachers from all over were together, where I served as a VIP/Talent Coordinator.

He was in line as I handled the VIP attendees and, as soon as we met face to face, he said: "Hi there, do you know that you have a calling on your life?" (I did not know him at that time, I had only heard of him and his group.)

"Yes, of course I do," was my reply. Then he shared that I was glowing and that my smile was healing. I said, "Oh wow, thank you!" not really thinking anything of it. I handed him his VIP package, we exchanged information, then we went our separate ways.

A few days later, he called: "Hi there, Lady."

And I said, "Hi there, Sir" –just to bounce the respect back. He told me he was about to tape in Atlanta and needed a lead soprano and asked if I could do the job for him? "Of course, I can, send me the track," I replied!

But shortly after, I thought of somebody else whom I felt was capable as well and called him back: "Hey, I can do the part, but I want to recommend someone else."

He said, "No, no, no, no, I want you for the part," but I persisted.

"Trust me, let me get her for you." I ended up giving that assignment to one of my childhood friends who can "sing her butt off," some coined her as a "Whitney Houston." He accepted my recommendation.

That was it, I thought, but he then called back a day later, saying, "Hey, my team and I still need you, could you do on-site management for us, and production?" I agreed because that is what I do anyway.

He added: "It's something about your glow."

Then came the turning point where I got my name *Lady LaDonna*. We were at sound check with other top gospel recording artists (anyone who was "someone" in the gospel industry was there), and he reminded me: "Just make sure that we follow our schedule . . ." I agreed. With the sound check finally over, I went back home for a while until time came to return for the live taping. I made it back ahead of time schedule to be sure the dressing rooms were prepped, and told the VIP registration director my name to locate on her roster, "My name is LaDonna Michellé."

She looked . . . then said, "I don't have that name here."

"Okay, well, Minister LaDonna?" Again, looking up and down the list she still could not locate it, so I proceeded to text my client, thinking my name had been omitted.

Before I could finish my text, the director said, "Wait, wait . . . I do see Lady LaDonna." I asked who was in connection with that name, and when she called out the artist's name, I assured her that it was who I was representing that evening.

She said, "Well, Lady LaDonna is on the roster."

I responded: "Well then, I guess I'm Lady LaDonna."

She gave me my credentials . . . and I walked in.

When I saw my client and asked about the name he had submitted to the roster, his reply was, "Your name is Lady LaDonna." That was the birth of *Lady LaDonna* in the industry. From that moment on, I was known as Lady LaDonna, becoming relevant in the public relations, music industry and other platforms. something was special about me ever since I was younger, but that gentleman really helped me to find my "Lady"!

I am very resilient and powerful in my own stance because I know my own worth. Yes, I stand in what God has called and purposed to me.

Lady LaDonna

Speaker • Author • Songstress

Through the passionate delivery of her signature brand of hope, love and empowerment, Lady LaDonna is transforming lives worldwide. The catalyst for the success of this noted speaker, author and songstress is her genuine love for people, combined with her desire to see them live fulfilled lives. After having worked behind the scenes in a plethora of arenas, Lady LaDonna (LaDonna Michellé) is gracefully stepping from beyond the shadows with the worldwide Amazon release of her life's story, *I Am D.I.V.A.: Destiny, Integrity, Victorious, Anointed*, November 14, 2020. She also looks forward to releasing recorded music "The Will to Love" in late Summer 2021.

Hailing from South Florida, Lady LaDonna studied Music Theory at Florida Memorial

University. She later studied at Beulah Heights University in Atlanta where she majored in Organizational Leadership/Administration; her minor was counseling. Lady LaDonna's professional experiences have afforded her an array of leadership opportunities in sacred and secular platforms. She utilized her amazing abilities in music and ministry on the sacred platform at one of Atlanta's largest mega churches, New Birth Missionary Baptist Church. She has also been just as active in outreach ministry in South Florida. Additionally, Lady LaDonna has 20+ years' ownership at BridgePointe Media & Entertainment, LLC, a well-established and respected public relations firm. In her spare time, Lady LaDonna enjoys international travel, boating, fishing and writing.

"The butterfly's beauty was developed in the cocoon, and so it is with our personal growth and development."

– Rev. Shalise Steele-Young

"An inspiring book for all women. A D.I.V.A. never faints, she leans in and WIN…"

**– Deborah Clemons,
CEO Infusions Blends**

Pure Thoughts Publishing LLC